Lhasa River

People's Republic of China

Beijing

Tibet
Autonomous
Region

Lhasa

Palace
on the
World's Rooftop

西藏布達

THE POTALA PALACE OF TIBET

拉宫

People's Art Publishing House, Shanghai   Joint Publishing Co., Hongkong

Photographs by
Zhang Hanyi
Yang Kelin
Li Jun
Dai Jiming
Kang Song
Yu Pengfei
Li Shuande
Design by
Ye Dao
James Chan
Art Editor:
Yin Wen
Project Editors:
Pan Shicong
Yang Keling
English translation by
Liu Biqi
Luo Zhaotian
Sun Liang
Ren Zhiji
Sun Zongbai
Translation Editors:
Chan Chiu Ming
Ho Kai

Compiled by
The Cultural Relics Administration Committee,
Tibet Autonomous Region

Published by
Joint Publishing Co. (Hongkong Branch)
9 Queen Victoria St., Hongkong
in association with
Shanghai People's Art Publishing House
No. 33, Lane 672, Changle Lu, Shanghai

English edition first published in May 1982
Second printing in April 1983
Third printing in February 1985

Colour separation by Evergreen Photolithography Co.
41, King's Road, 1st Floor, North Point, Hongkong

Printed in Hongkong by
C & C Joint Printing Co. (H.K.) Ltd.
75 Pau Chung St., Kowloon, Hongkong

ISBN 962·04·0196·4

Contents

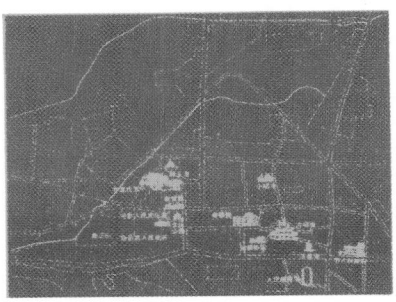

The Potala Palace

by Deng Ruiling

The Potala Palace, situated on the Red Hill in the northwest of the Municipality of Lhasa, People's Republic of China, is the largest and the best preserved massif of anicent Tibetan architecture extant today. Covering the whole face of the hill from its foot at more than 3,600 metres above sea level, the main portion of the building rises in thirteen storeys to more than 110 metres in height, and the whole edifice measures well over 360 metres in width. Built entirely of wood and stone, this immense towering structure comprises a maze of rooms and compartments heaped up in seeming irregularity and intricate workmanship. Crowned with glistening golden roofs and soaring eaves, it is surrounded by steep walls overhanging flights of stone steps winding to the gates. When viewed from a distance, the whole complex presents an impressive picture of harmony, grandeur and magnificence beyond description. Truly it is a masterpiece of Tibetan architectural beauty and an embodiment of the creative genius of the Tibetan working people.

The Potala Palace was built in the middle of the 17th century by order of a great personage in Tibetan history, the 5th Dalai Lama, Ngawang Lobzang Gyatso. According to records, construction work began in the year of the Wood Cock of the 11th Rabjune (a Rabjune is a sixty-year cycle in the Tibetan calendar), i.e., 1645 A.D. This was the fourth year after the 5th Dalai Lama, as the head of the Gelugpa Sect and with the military aid of the Qosot Mongols from Qinghai, had vanquished his rival and supporter of the Karmapa Sect, the Tsangpa Khan of Tsang. It took fully three years to complete the part of the building known as the White Palace to which he removed from the Drepung Monastery. Ever since, the White Palace has become the official residence of all his successors.

Potala, a phonetic translation of the Sanskrit Potalaka, is the name of a hill on the southern coast of anicent India. Monk Xuan Zhuang of the Tang Dynasty more accurately transcribed it as 'Po Ta Lo Ka Hill' in his *Records on the West Regions of the Tang Dynasty (Datang xiyu ji)*, in which he gave not only an account of its topographical features but also the myth that the Boddhisattva Avalokitesvara used to make it a place of his sojourn. And as the abode of the said Boddhisattva, the name in translation was further contracted to 'Po Tuo.' According to the Tibetan historical work *A Happy Feast of the Sages*, *(Mkhas ba'i dga' stor)* it was king Songtsan Gambo who first built a fort-palace on the Red Hill. As Tibetan Buddhists traditionally regarded him as the incarnation of Boddhisattva Avalokitesvara, the hill came to be known as Potala. And according to *The Precious Tree of Perfect Bliss (Dpag bsam ljon bZang)* by Sumpa Khanpo, the fort-palace was once destroyed by thunder in the time of king Khrisong Detsan. Hence, the present palace was rebuilt on the ruins of the old site of the 7th century.

Now in choosing a site of such historical backgrounds for reconstruction the 5th Dalai Lama proved himself a man of subtle political acumen. Since there had been in Tibet the old tradition about Songtsan Gambo being the incarnation of the Boddhisattva Avalokitesvara, the 5th Dalai Lama proclaimed himself also an incarnation of the Boddhisattva, thus emulating the historical significance of the famous king. And by restoring the palace at Potala, the alleged abode of the Boddhisattva, he was comparing his own efforts in subduing the remnant Karmapa Sect and in unifying U, Tsang and Ngari with the illustrious deeds of the founder of the Tubo Dynasty by the implication that they were actually 'the two merged in one.' Thus the place was destined to be not only a hermitage for retirement and meditation of the head of a religious sect but also a centre for the feudal government of Tibet during the last three hundred years or more.

The Red Palace which forms the central portion of the whole structure was mainly built between 1690 and 1693 under Depa Sanggye Gyatso. It was built in the memory of the 5th Dalai Lama after his decease. And here is ensconced the huge chorten wherein his remains were preserved.

The construction of the whole palace lasting over several decades may be said to have been completed in the main by the end of the 17th century. It was estimated that seven thousand artisans took part in the building of the Red Palace alone, while those employed in hewing timbers and stones from the forest and quarry were to be counted in tens of thousands. This gives a sufficient idea to the magnitude of corvée labour and material resource used to be exacted from the people by the 5th Dalai Lama and Sanggye Gyatso, backed as they were by both the central authority of the Qing Dynasty and the military prowess of the Qosot Mongols. It also indicates, nonetheless, a thriving social economy under stable political unity which made it possible for the people to supply the necessary man power and resource over such a long period.

At that time there were also monk artisans of Han nationality who came from the inland to join in the planning and construction. So while the basic structure of the palace is a combination of a residence and a fort, which accords with the Tibetan tradition, it has also assimilated many decorative features like the elaborate beams and rafters, corbel brackets, gold roofings, painted ceilings, etc., characteristic of Han architecture.

In the numerous corridors and porticos, mural paintings done by famous Tibetan artists vividly portray scenes of the toiling mass while construction was in progress, leaving us a most valuable and authentic record on the history of the palace.

In 1661 A.D., when the 5th Dalai Lama was just at the zenith of his power, the Jesuit Father Grueber and his companion travelled from Beijing to Lhasa via Qinghai. As the Potala then consisted of only the White Palace, he left behind a sketch as he saw it, perhaps the first sketch ever made. Fifty-five years later, another Jesuit missionary named Desideri arrived at Lhasa, and he noticed that the palace comprised both the White Palace and the Red Palace. This was what he wrote: 'Now this palace occupies the whole top of the rock of Potala, but in old days it was smaller, as shown by the drawing made by the Rev. Albert D'Orville and Rev. Johan Grueber of our society ....'

In the time of Emperor Kang Xi, many Han artisans participated in the construction of the palace and many imperial envoys must have left their footprints on the stone steps leading to the White Palace. But it was in 1720 that a military officer named Li Fengcai in the expedition force to expel the Jungar Mongols from Lhasa explicitly mentioned Potala as the name of the place where the Living Buddha was enthroned, with a description of its fearful images of worship and its treasuries overflowing with wealth. A contemporary civil officer, Jiao Yingqi, after a short stay of eight days in Lhasa also remarked in his journals about the Dalai Lama's magnificent palace with words like 'Hundreds of towering buildings, many storeys high, with beautiful adornments in shining gold that defy description,' though he did not mention its name.

Since the time of Sanggye Gyatso, the palace had been extended by successive generations of Dalai Lamas especially in the 18th century. And since it was the residence of Dalai Lamas and the administative centre of the Tibet Region, important religious ceremonies and festivals took place here every year. All important political functions were also held here such as the formal installation of each young Dalai Lama when the Resident Amban of the Qing Court presided over the ceremony in the East Hall to inaugurate the Dalai into office. Imperial edicts, royal letters of appointment, gold diplomas and gold seals issued by the Central Government to the high clerical and lay officials together with religious utensils and plaques bearing the Emperor's handwriting were preserved here, as was also the memorial tablet dedicated to the Emperor in the four languages of Han, Tibetan, Manchurian and Mongolian. All these bear testimony to the authority vested in the Tibetan leadership headed by the Dalai Lama and ratified by the Central Government as to their being legitimate rulers of Tibet.

In the White Palace, the Dalai Lama and his clerical attendants lived, prayed and supervised the daily administration, while the main part of the Red Palace is reserved, among a number of prayer halls, for the eight chortens covered with shining gold, pearls and gems in which the embalmed bodies of the deceased Dalai Lamas were preserved.

Potala is also a veritable museum of fine arts, the best talents of Tibet being represented here in sculpture, painting, printing, calligraphy and other fine arts and crafts. Especially valuable are the mural paintings in the numerous corridors and porticos. There are paintings on religious subjects as well as scenes from the daily life of the Tibetan people. Fine pictures about the story of the

Princesses Wen Cheng and Jin Cheng of the Tang Dynasty are to be seen in the corridors and the East Audience Hall of the White Palace, demonstrating the genuine affection of the Tibetan people to the two princesses who devoted themselves to promoting cultural exchange and harmonious relation between the Han and Tibetan nationalities. In the West Audience Hall are paintings depicting the audience granted by the Qing Emperor Shun Zhi to the 5th Dalai Lama at Beijing and that of Emperor Guang Xu and Empress Dowager Ci Xi to the 13th Dalai Lama, indicating the Dalai Lamas' subordination to the Emperors.

Towards the end of the 19th century, the Potala like many other places of historical importance in China experienced defilement by imperialism. In the year 1904, it was in the main hall of the Potala Palace that, under the threat of British military power, Tibetan officials were forced to sign the 'Lhasa Convention.'

This imposing structure on the Red Hill had stood as a historical witness to the many political vicissitudes which Tibet had gone through in the past till the day of democratic reform. Now, cleansed of all stains of its former humiliation, tyranny and iniquity, it is restored to the people.

Since liberation, the State Council of the People's Republic of China has given the greatest attention to this world-renowned old Tibetan architecture and allocated special funds every year for its repair and maintenance. In 1961, Potala was officially declared one of the old historical sites under state protection. It is now a unique historical museum and is drawing an ever increasing number of visitors, both native and foreign, to come each year.

Deng Ruiling, of the Manchu nationality, was born in Beijing in 1925.

He was graduated from the History Dept. and later, from the Research Institute of Peking University.

He is now an assistant research fellow of the Nationality Research Institute of the Chinese Academy of Social Science. His present position is Deputy Director of the Research Centre of the institute.

The Story of the Potala Palace

by Dongar Lobzand Chinlei

Translated from Tibetan

by Trashi Wangdu & Chang Fengxuan

The Potala Palace is the creation of the industrious and ingenious Tibetan working people who successfully employed their remarkable cultural and artistic heritage. It embodies in itself the technical and artistic accomplishments of civil engineering, palatial layout, sculpture, casting, mural painting and interior decoration of the Tibetan culture and is one of the wonders among the world's buildings.

The palace is a mammoth piece of architecture built in the traditional Tibetan style, with a history of over 1,000 years. In early 7th century, the wise Tsanpo (king) Songtsan Gambo (617-650, unifier and first king of unified Tibet) came of age and took the reigns of government. He built a house on the Marpo Ri Hill (Red Hill), which shape was like a sleeping elephant. This was later to become the Chogye Drupha (Meditation Palace for the Religious Lords), situated at the northern part of the hill. Songtsan Gambo took to wife a Nepalese and a Han princess. When Princess Wen Cheng from the Tang Court was on her way to Tibet, he built another palace on the Marpo Ri Hill, and named it the Khritse Marpo (Palace of the Red-canopied Throne), alias the Potala (Abode of Avalokitesvara). This is how the Potala came into being according to historical records. The Red Palace, as it was later called, was damaged during the reign of Mangsong Mangtsan, and later was destroyed by lightning fire during the reign of Khrisong Detsan in the 8th century. But a picture of the Red Palace is preserved intact in a fresco inside the main entrance of the Jokhang Temple in Lhasa.

After this, Tibet experienced a long period of turmoil and war, and the palaces became run-down and dilapidated. During the 12th century, Kardampa Geshay preached Buddhist scriptures on the Potala Hill, and afterwards, Master Tsong Khapa, the founder of the Karmapa and Gelugpa of Tshurphu, also gave sermons on Buddhist sutras there. Obviously, the buildings on top of the hill were no longer palaces at the time, but houses for preaching Buddhism. During the consecutive rule of Phamo Drupa and Karmapa of the Kargyupa Sect over U (Anterior Tibet), temporary imperial palaces were set up in Lhasa. And Ngawang Trashi Drapa, the 11th king of the Phadru Dynasty, built a temporary imperial residence named the Gangri Karpo (Palace of the Snow-capped Mountain) in Qüsü, thus guarding the strategic point overlooking U, Tsang and Lhoka regions. He gave his former residence, Dokhang Ngenmo (Green Rock Palace) in the Drepung Monastery, to the 2nd Dalai Lama. Later, the Dalai Lama changed the name of the Dokhang Ngenmo into the Gandan Phodrang, which became the holy residence of the 2nd, 3rd, 4th and 5th Dalai Lamas.

In early 17th century, the Qosot tribe of the Oelot Mongols invaded Tibet. They overthrew the rule of Karma Tanhwei Wangpu and helped the 5th Dalai Lama to the throne. The 5th Dalai Lama found that living in the Gandan Phodrang Palace within the Drepung Monastery was an infringement of the regulations of the monastery. But he also considered the Gangri Karpo Palace in Qüsü too far away from the three great monasteries in Lhasa. Therefore he built, in 1645-1648, a new palace in the eastern side of the Potala Hill according to the design of the Red Palace of Songtsan Gambo as preserved in the fresco in the Jokhang Temple. He named the new palace the White Palace. The reason for choosing the Potala Hill as the site for his new palace was that it was the place where Songtsan Gambo set up his first government after unifying Tibet, and it was there that Songtsan Gambo married the Nepalese princess and Princess Wen Cheng from the Tang Court. Furthermore, it was situated at the place which for centuries had been the centre of friendly exchange in political, economic and cultural fields among various nationalities. The Potala was within easy reach of the three great monasteries in Lhasa, and, therefore, convenient in keeping a tight hold on the state and the church. So, after the completion of the White Palace, the 5th Dalai Lama moved his residence from the Gandan Phodrang Palace in the Drepung Monastery to the Zimchung Nyierh Palace (Sunlight Palace) on top of the Potala Hill. From then on, this palace has become the living quarters of successive Dalai Lamas. The Audience Hall on the ground floor of the White Palace was the place where various Dalai Lamas attended to state and church affairs. The frescoes in this hall, which still retain their bright colours, were painted by

Choying Gyatsho, a famous painter sent by the 4th Panchen Lama from the Trashi Lhumpo Monastery. The palace also housed the Kashag (the Council of Ministers) and the Yitshang (the Secretariat) set up during the early years of the Qing Dynasty. The White Palace was kept in good repair and underwent several renovations during the reigns of the 8th, 9th, 12th and 13th Dalai Lamas.

The central part of the Potala Palace is the Red Palace. It was build under the general supervision of Depa (Chief Administrator) Sanggye Gyatso. Construction work began in 1690, the year of the Iron Horse in the Tibetan calendar, eight years after the death of the 5th Dalai Lama. It took four years to complete the work. The builders tore down half of the western part of the original White Palace and extended the former Red Palace on its eastern, southern and western sides. Conforming to the Tibetan tradition, the palace has thirteen storeys and bears the features of both palaces and temples in its outward appearance; while the interior was built strictly according to the design of Tantric cosmography.

The top floor of the Red Palace, decorated in conformity with the design of the orthodox Gelugpa Sect, was the living quarters of the Dalai Lama. The floor below are the Hall of the Medicine King, the Lama Hall, the Hall of the God of the Hans, the Hall of the Bronze Buddha of Khotan, etc. Further below are the Prayer Hall and four other great halls at its four sides. The walls of the Prayer Hall are decorated with frescoes depicting the life story of the 5th Dalai Lama. On the walls of the corridor outside the Prayer Hall are frescoes presenting the life of Depa Sanggye Gyatso. Frescoes are also found in other halls telling the life stories of Masters Atisha and Dromtonpa, teacher and disciple, of the Gelugpa Sect. These frescoes were painted by Tandzin Norbu and other Tibetan master painters of the time. Apart from the eight chortens containing salt-dried and embalmed remains of eight Dalai Lamas, there preserved in the palace are 246 scrolls of paintings in gold, 65 colour scrolls depicting the life story of the 5th Dalai Lama, 46 privately handed-down scrolls, 615 Buddhist sutras in gold characters, the *Kangyur* and the *Tangyur*, also gold-charactered, and other valuable books on medicine, calendar and history as well as biographies and anthologies.

In building the Red Palace craftsmen of many trades were employed; among them are painters, engravers, founders, mosaicists, goldsmiths, coppersmiths, ironsmiths, spinners, tanners, greasers, mortar mixers and stonemasons. The authorities also enlisted corvée labourers from serfs of the households of seven high-ranking officials, thirteen aristocratic households and monastic plantations. Craftsmen of Han, Mongolian and Nepalese nationalities were invited to participate in this grandiose project. According to historical records, a total of 6,743 Tibetan, Han, Mongolian and Nepalese craftsmen worked jointly in building this magnificent and awe-inspiring palace in traditional Tibetan architectural style.

The layout of the palace was done with superb skill that puts nature to shame. Built on a hill shaped like a sleeping elephant, it is a building complex in which the White and Red Palaces are ingeniously grouped together. After nearly three hundred years, the palace is still in good condition, magnificent and splendid as ever. Obviously, without a period of political solidarity and stability and a fairly developed economy, it would be impossible to launch such a giant undertaking. After the peaceful liberation of the Tibetan Region, the people's government listed the Potala Palace among the first class of cultural relics to be put under state protection. Large funds are allocated every year by the state for the repair and renovation of the Potala.

The Potala Palace is admired by people of all nationalities in China. It is the fruit of the collective intelligence of many brilliant statesmen, clever craftsmen and industrious working people of different historical periods. It is the pride of the Chinese nation.

Dongar Lobzand Chinlei, born in Milin County of the Tibetan Autonomous Region in 1927, is of the Tibetan nationality. He is the living Buddha of the Dongar Monastery in Gongbu Region of Tibet. He once studied in Sela Monastery of Lhasa and got the title of dge-bshes (equivalent to a doctoral degree in Buddhism) after passing the final examination and in the meanwhile got a degree of Lha-rim-pa and Sngags-rim-pa of the Tri-monasteries.

Plates and Notes

Exterior View

The Potala Palace is a pearl on the Tibetan plateau. Miles away from Lhasa, one can see its majestic contour soaring into the sky and towering above the Red Hill by the Lhasa River. The Palace is one of the highest castles of the world.

Early in the 7th century, King Songtsan Gambo established the Tubo Dynasty with Lhasa as its capital. In 641 A.D. the second emperor of the Tang Dynasty, Li Shimin, sent Princess Wen Cheng of the royal house to Tibet to be married to King Songtsan Gambo. As recorded in both Han and Tibetan chronicles, Songtsan Gambo decided to build a castle for the princess in order to win the admiration of posterity, and he chose the Red Hill as the site of construction. The palaces and shrines built in that period had mostly been destroyed. They were reconstructed on a larger scale in the 17th century and repeatedly repaired afterwards till we see them as they are today.

The Potala Palace, standing on the summit of a mountain and rising against the sky, presents a magnificent spectacle of lofty grandeur no matter viewed from what angle. It is the pride of Lhasa, the City of Sunshine.

1

1. The Potala Palace
The Potala Palace is situated on the Red Hill around Lhasa, capital of the Tibet Autonomous Region. The Palace is named after the Hill which has been respectfully called the Potala Hill by the Buddhists.

2. Front View of the Palace

The entire palace, from the east end to the west end, is over 360 metres in length, covering an area of more than 100,000 square metres with massive groups of red and white terraces. The Red Palace is located in the centre, flanked by the White Palace on both sides. The former houses the chortens of deceased Dalai Lamas as well as halls and chapels for worshipping Buddha used by successive generations of Dalai Lamas, while the latter is comprised of living chambers and sitting rooms of the Dalai Lamas and various kinds of rooms for the monks.

3

3. Rear View of the Palace
Building palaces on hills is traditional in Tibetan architecture. The foundation stones of the Potala Palace are laid deep into rocks, and the stone walls are embedded in the precipice. Taking advantages of the natural environment, the building seems to have grown out of the crags.

4. Naga Temple and Pool
5. Nage Temple and Pool
This pool lies behind the Palace. When the Potala Palace was reconstructed in 1645 by order of the 5th Dalai Lama, the workers dug up clods of earth behind the hill to make cement for the walls. After the completion of the building, there appeared on the spot a deep pool like a small lake wherein the Dragon King Temple was erected, hence the name of the pool.

4

6

6-7. Side Views of the Potala Palace
The Palace is a 13-storeyed building rising 117.19 metres high. Its grand contour can be seen at a great distance.

9

8. Palace Walls
Since the whole building is a structure of earth and stone, the double walls in the palace are as thick as two to five metres, some of which are made solid and anti-seismic by pouring molten copper into them.

9. The Stone Steps
The winding steps are built along the hillside with myriads of stone blocks.

10

10. The Spot Where the Officials Dismounted
Behind the Palace there is a road along which local officials in Tibet
in the past used to ride on horseback to pay homage to the Dalai
Lama (cf. picture 3). At this round fort officials of the sixth rank
used to dismount to show respect.

11. Round Forts
The round forts at the eastern and western corners of the Palace
belong to its outer premises, symbolizing the sun and the moon. This
is the eastern fort.

12. The East Gate

This is the only gate through which the Potala Palace is accessible to visitors.

13. Monks' Chambers

This is the western section of the Palace, which used to be the dwelling place of over 100 monks. It is called 'Drakhang' in Tibetan, meaning chambers for the monks.

14. The East Terrace

This terrace is called 'Deyangshar' in Tibetan. It is built halfway up the hill at an elevation of over 70 metres, covering an area of 1,600 square metres. Religious rituals and performances with songs and dances used to be held here on festive occasions.

Palaces and Cultural Relics

The Potala combines halls, shrines, and chortens into one architectural entity. Since the 5th Dalai Lama, Lobzang Gyatso, moved into the palace in 1653, it has been the residence of Dalai Lamas as well as being the centre of religious and political activities. The building and reconstruction of the Potala Palace not only displayed the fine tradition and unique style of ancient Tibetan architecture, but also assimilated the characteristics of Han and Nepalese architecture. According to historical records, when the Palace was first built in the 7th century on the Red Hill by order of Songtsan Gambo, many Han artisans were employed. Likewise, when the Palace underwent reconstruction in the 17th century, monks from the inland participated in designing the project, and Han workers joined in the efforts of building. As a special favour, the Qing Emperor Kang Xi dispatched a group of Han and Manchu artisans to Tibet to help with the construction. The neighbouring country Nepal also sent a lot of craftsmen to take part in the project. The building of the Potala Palace, therefore, is a story of national co-operation and international cultural exchange in the history of Chinese architecture.

15. The Song Ge Guo Corridor
Ascending the stone steps from the East Terrace, one will reach the Song Ge Guo Corridor, the passage through which visitors go to various halls and shrines upstairs. Along the corridor are tall carved beams and pillars. Painted on the walls are exquisite murals.

16. Gold Benba (Gold Urn)

To prevent the Mongolian and Tibetan aristocracy from manipulating the reincarnation of the Living Buddhas, the central government of the Qing Dynasty decreed in 1792 that two gold benbas be available in Beijing and Lhasa respectively. Whenever there were more than one reincarnated child to become Living Buddhas like the Dalai and Panchen Lamas, the names of the children concerned were engraved on small ivory sticks put in the gold benbas and one of the sticks was to be drawn under the supervision of the Resident Amban in Lhasa or Beijing .The holy child with his name drawn was the legitimate successor and would be inaugurated by holding a grand ceremony in the East Hall.

17. The East Hall

This is the largest hall in the White Palace, built in 1645. Here the Resident Amban (Governor of Tibet) appointed by the Qing court used to preside over the grand ceremonies of officially installing each young Dalai Lama and inaugurating him into holy office. Other important religious and political functions were also held in this hall.

18. The West Hall

This is the largest hall in the Red Palace with a floor space of over 680 square metres. It is the shrine housing the chorten of the 5th Dalai Lama. A plaque is hung here bearing the inscription written by Emperor Qian Long in the 25th year of his reign: 'Holy Spot of Emerging Lotus.' There are mural paintings on all the walls, among which is a sequence depicting the life of the 5th Dalai Lama, highlighting the audience granted him by Emperor Shun Zhi in Beijing in the year 1652.

19. The Plaque Bearing Imperial Inscription Granted by Emperor Qian Long

20. Carved Pillars

In the main halls and chapels in the Palace, there are lots of pillars carved with consummate workmanship in a unique style. The Tibetan craftsmen first carved varied patterns and designs on pieces of wood, then stuck them onto the pillars, and finally bound them with brass hoops.

21

21. Giant Elephant
Below the Buddha's seat there are decorations of wood carvings like the giant elephant, the holy horse, the peacock, and birds of symbiosis. These lifelike images are wrought with superb craftsmanship.

22. Holy Horse
23. Peacock
24. Birds of Symbiosis

22

23

24

25. Lintel

27

26. Carved Brackets
The carved patterns on the brackets are comprised of 13 layers,
symbolizing 13 meritorious services rendered by Sakyamuni,
founder of Buddhism.

27. Carved Brackets

28

29

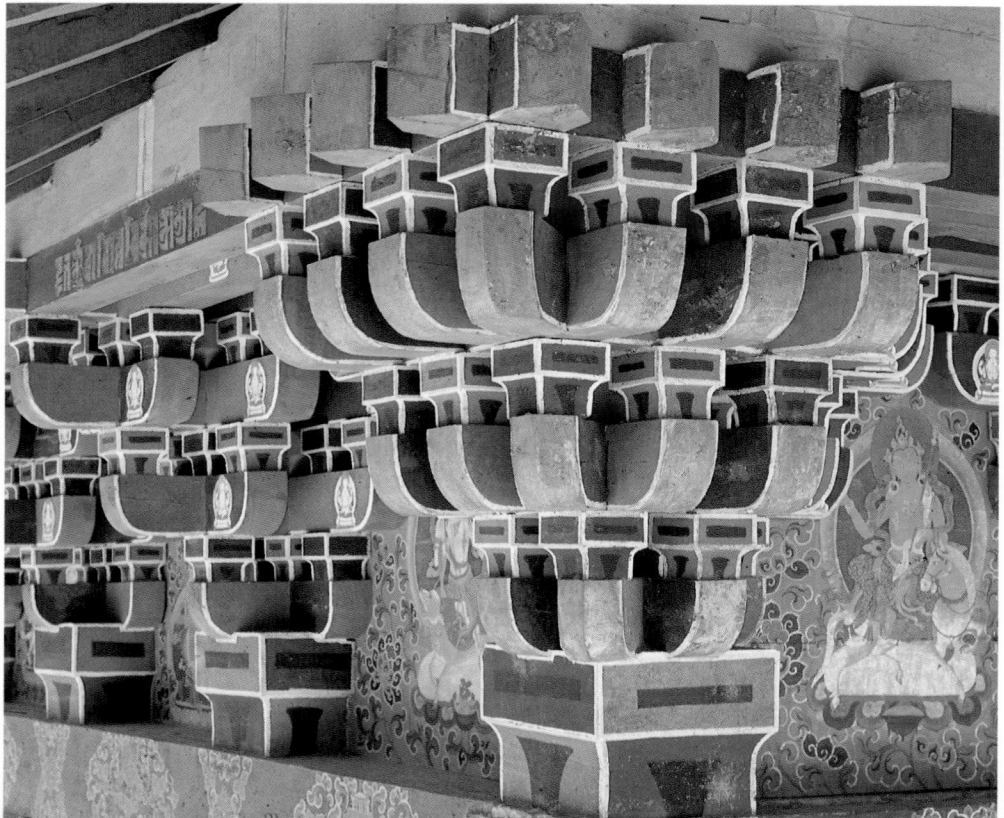

30

28. Bracket System Decorated with the Images of Tiger and Other Beasts

29. Pig-Nose-Shaped Bracketing System

This peculiar bracketing system on golden roofs is not only for ornamental purpose but also helps to ward off violent winds and protect the building.

30. Trunk-shaped Bracketing System

31. The White Pagoda

Legend has it that the White Pagoda was erected during the reign of Songtsan Gambo. It is the earliest building on the Red Hill. Beneath the Pagoda lies the top of the Hill, which is now just in the middle of the Potala Palace.

32. Corridor with Carved Pillars

33. Gold Seal and Gold Plate Engraved with Imperial Edicts

As a rule the Qing government granted gold seals and gold plate diplomas to successive generations of the Dalai Lamas, The gold seal in this picture was granted by Qing court to the 5th Dalai Lama on the occasion of conferring a grand title on him. The gold plate was granted to the 11th Dalai Lama in 1841.

34. Portrait of Emperor Qian Long and Seat for the Longevity Tablet Dedicated to Emperor Kang Xi
Both the tablet seat granted to the 7th Dalai Lama and the imperial portrait granted to the 8th Dalai Lama were set up in the highest hall in the Potala Palace, the 'Sasong Langjie,' which means the 'Three Splendid Realms': the Dragon Realm of the nether world, the Human Realm on earth, and the Holy Realm in Heaven. Successive generations of the Dalai Lamas used to come here on New Year's Day and the Emperors' birthdays to pay respect to the royal portrait and tablet.

35. The Saint's Chapel (Phagpa Lhakhang)
This chapel is one of the early buildings in the Palace that remain intact today. The Buddhist statue enshrined here is said to be the patron saint of King Songtsan Gambo. A plaque is hung high above the door of the chapel with an inscription written by Emperor Tong Zhi: 'Futian Miaoguo' ('Blissful Soil Nourishing Miraculous Fruits').

36. Gilt Double-Knockers
37. Gate Leading to the West Hall

37

39

38. The Western Sunshine Hall
This hall was constructed in the period of the 13th Dalai Lama.

39. The Eastern Sunshine Hall
Located in the highest position in the White Palace, the residential quarters of the Dalai Lamas are divided into two sections: the eastern and the western. As there is plenty of sunlight in the halls, they are called the Eastern Sunshine Hall and the Western Sunshine Hall respectively. Both halls house chapels, drawing rooms, libraries of Buddhist scriptures, and living chambers, which are all furnished luxuriously. The gold and silver utensils, jewellery, curios and relics belonging to the Dalai Lamas are still kept in these halls. In the old days, only officials above the fourth rank were qualified to be granted audience here by the Dalai Lamas.

40

41

40. Agate Bowl
41. Gold Pot and Jade Bowl
The gold pot is made of pure gold weighing 4,000 grams.

42. Living Chamber of the Dalai Lamas
The 5th Dalai Lama and all his successors lived here.

Mural
Paintings

Mural painting is an integral part of the architecture of the Potala Palace. There are colourful and exquisite murals on the walls of every hall, every chapel, and every corridor. In addition, there is a rich treasure of scroll paintings in the Palace, hence it is just like a gallery of fine arts.

The subject matter of such a great variety of murals may be classified into two main categories: the portraits and biographical pictures of historical figures, and pictorial stories adapted from Buddhist scriptures. The Tibetan painters often use the techniques of vertical view and diversified perspective as well as the methods of single line and plane colouring; they use a single colour mixed with multiple colours to present a sharp contrast and thereby mould picturesque images.

As related in the autobiography of the 5th Dalai Lama, the murals in the Potala Palace were first painted in 1648 with the joint efforts of 32 Tibetan painters over a period of more than ten years. These murals have been re-painted time and again over the past 300 years or so, and many new paintings have been added to form the present spectacle. Most of these have been explained in words so that they have become very important data for studying the development of Tibetan history and art.

43

43. The Gallery on the First Floor of the West Hall
In this gallery there are 698 mural paintings on different subject
matters and done with fine brushwork. It is the richest collection of
murals in the Palace.

44. Murals in the West Hall
Employing the method of depicting various incidents in a serial
form, the Tibetan painters portrayed a good number of the personal
experiences of the 5th Dalai Lama in a single painting. It is,
therefore, like a pictorial story. The big portrait of King Songtsan
Gambo in the centre reflects the veneration towards and memory of
the King on the part of the 5th Dalai Lama.

45

45. The 5th Dalai Lama blessing the Emperor Shun Zhi
46. The Thirteenth Dalai Lama Being Granted
Audience by Emperor Guang Xu and Empress Dowager
Ci Xi in Beijing
These are the scenes of the 13th Dalai Lama, Thutan Gyatso, being
received in audience by the Qing rulers in Beijing in 1908: upper
picture shows Emperor Guang Xu entertaining the 13th Dalai
Lama at a banquet in the Qin Zheng (Assiduous Administration)
Hall in the imperial palace; lower picture shows the 13th Dalai
Lama paying homage to Empress Dowager Ci Xi. (Murals in the
second floor of the chorten hall of the 13th Dalai Lama)

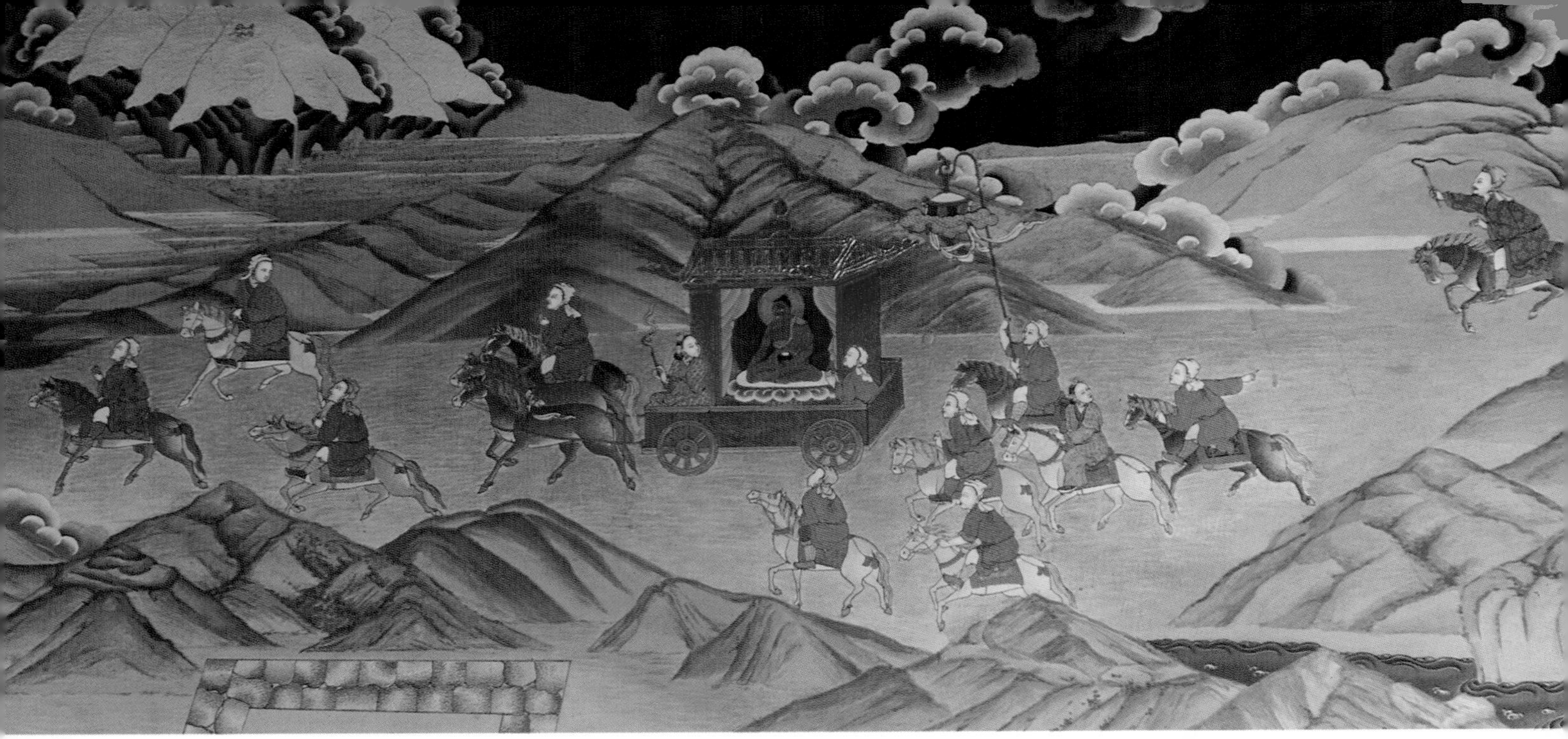
47

48
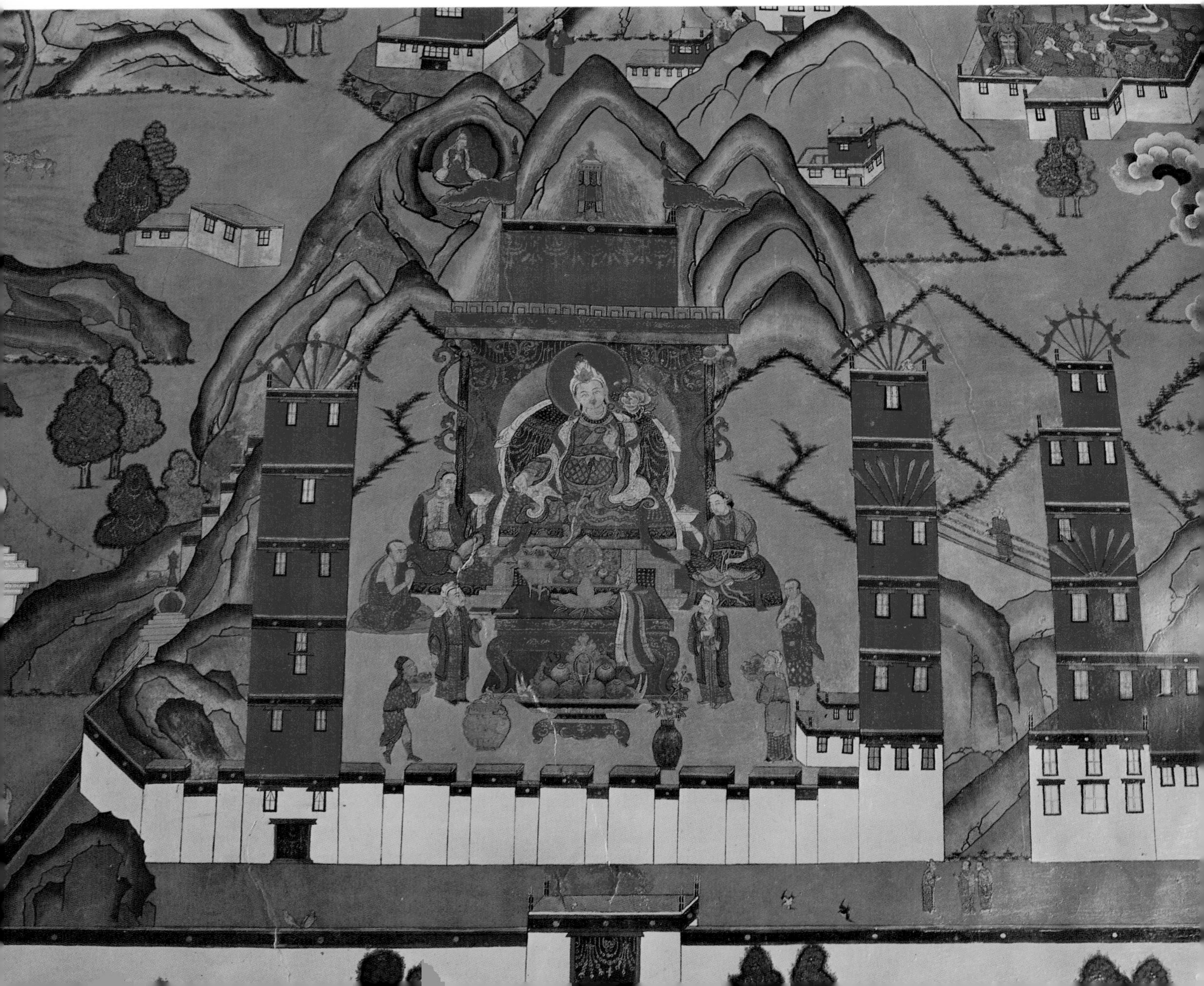

47. Princess Wen Cheng Coming to Tibet

When the Princess came to Tibet, it was recorded, she brought an image of Sakyamuni in the royal carriage. (In this picture the Princess sat at the fore in the vehicle.) Accompanying her were a large entourage and a great number of artisans of different professions such as papermakers, brewers and builders. Consequently, the techniques of productive labour and cultural achievements of the Han people were introduced into Tibet with the coming of Princess Wen Cheng. The marriage between members of the Tang and Tubo royal houses promoted a close relationship of kindred affinity. (Mural in the Song Ge Guo Corridor)

48. Palaces on the Red Hill during the Reign of Songtsan Gambo

As recorded in the annals, the palaces at that time were highrising but limited in area space, with flat roofs and in the shape of a pagoda. Bows, arrows, spears and swords were installed on the rooftops. Trenches were dug below the forts. There was an iron bridge connecting the king's palace and that of the queen to facilitate communication. (Mural in the Song Ge Guo Corridor)

49. Princess Jin Cheng

After Princess Wen Cheng, Jin Cheng, another princess of the Tang royal house, adopted daughter of Emperor Zhong Zong, was sent to Tibet to be married to King Khride Tsutsan, thereby further promoted friendly relations as well as economic and cultural exchanges between the Han and Tibetan nationalities. (Mural in the East Hall)

50. Flying Apsaras
Apsaras are deities which fly freely in paradise. They are attendants
of the Buddha. (Mural in the gallery on the first floor of the West
Hall)

51. The Heavenly King of the East
This portrait of Dhrtarastra, Heavenly King of the East, was painted
in the 17th century. (5 metres high, 3.55 metres wide. Mural in
the Song Ge Guo Corridor)

52

53

52. Reconstruction of the Red Palace in the Potala Palace

This fresco shows the scene of reconstructing the Potala Palace in the 17th century. In 1645, the 5th Dalai Lama issued a decree of mobilization for the reconstruction of the Potala Palace. By 1648 the building of the White Palace had been completed, thereupon the 5th Dalai Lama moved from the Drepung Monastery to the Potala Palace. After he passed away, the project of reconstructing the Red Palace and the chorten for him started, which was basically completed in 1693. A blank stela was set up in front of the Palace to commemorate the 5th Dalai Lama. (Mural in the gallery on the first floor of the West Hall)

53. Reconstruction of the Red Palace in the Potala (Detail)

This is a section of the above-mentioned picture (top right corner). The boatmen are steering a cattlehide boat loaded with stones along the boisterous Lhasa River. The huge stone in the boat was to be erected as the blank stela still standing in front of the Palace today.

ৡৢ৹ ঝৢৢ৾ড়ৢৢৄৢৢ৾ঀৢড়৾ৢ৾৻ৢঀৢ৾৾৾ৢ৾৾ঀ৾৾ঀ৾৾৾

ৠৢ৾৾ৢৢৢ৾৾৾ৢ৾৾ৢৢ৾ৢৢ৾৾৾ৢ৾৾ৠৢ৾৾৾৾৾

54. Celebrating the
Completion of the Red
Palace (Detail)

65

55. Celebrating the Completion of the Red Palace
Upon the completion of the Red Palace in the Potala Palace, Depa Sanggye
Gyatso held a grand ceremony to celebrate the occasion. This is one of the
scenes: artisans of different nationalities participating in the project are engaged
in various games like archery, racing, weight lifting, wrestling, and so on.
(Mural in the gallery on the first floor of the West Hall)

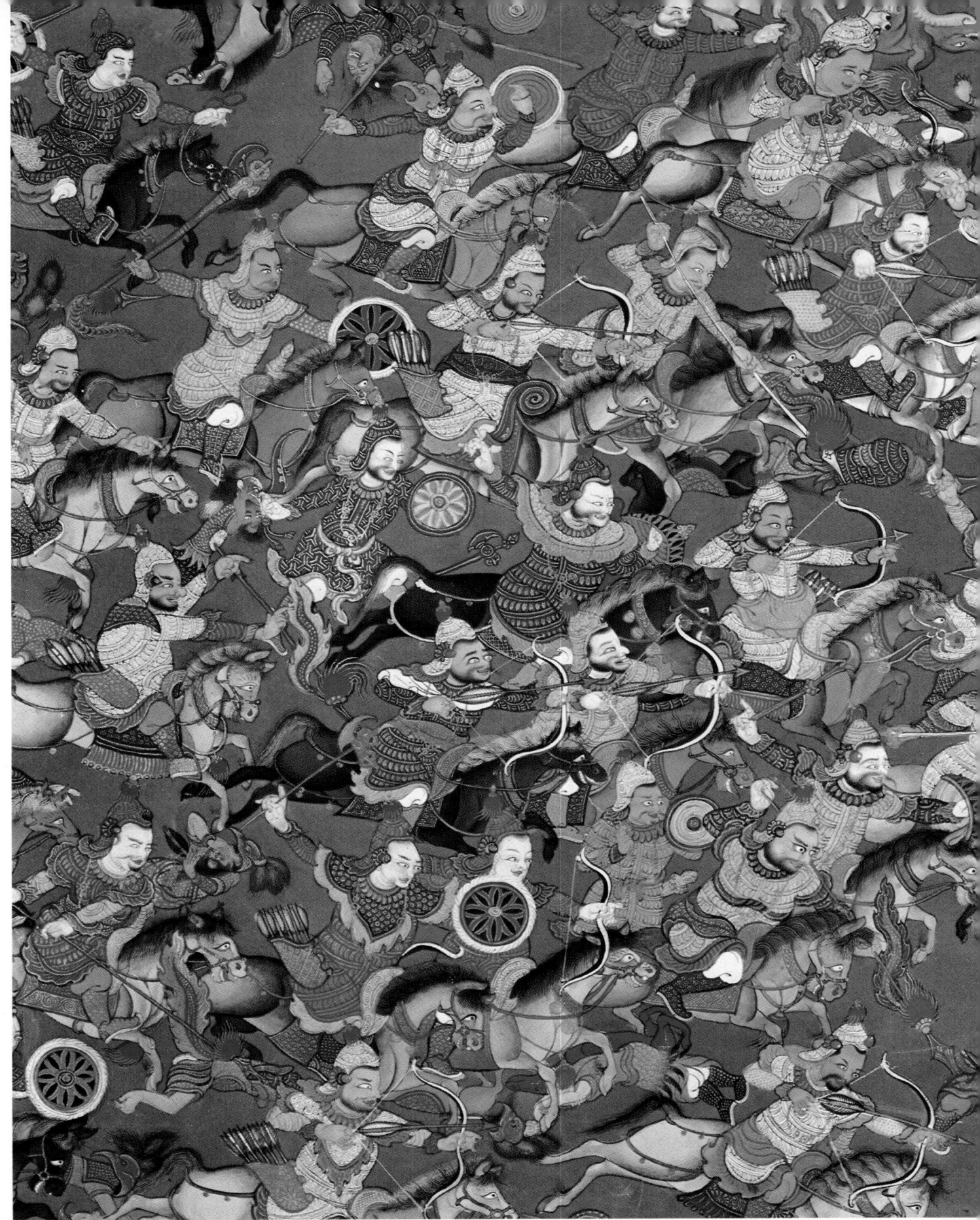

56. The 'Shangpala' Myth (Detail)
This is a detail of the large Thangka drawn on the 'Shangpala'
myth: an imaginary scene of fierce fighting in a future war.

57-58. Thangka (Scroll Painting) — Arhats

Thangka is the name of Tibetan scroll painting done on silk or cloth. There are different kinds of this genre: painted, woven or embroidered. Like the frescos, they reflect the artistic achievements of the Tibetan art of painting. Here are two pieces of Thangka which comprise portraits of arhats (Buddhist saints).

58

Sculptures

There are many sculptures of various kinds in the Potala Palace, including the statues of prominent figures in Tibetan history such as King Songtsan Gambo, Lutongtsan, Tsong Khapa, the 5th Dalai Lama, and so forth. Moreover, there are a great number of Buddhist and other religious images. All of them look grave and imposing in a solemn atmosphere.

There are certain rules and principles of painting and sculpture expounded in sutras contained in the Tibetan version of the *Tripitaka* canon, but they do not strictly restrain the Tibetan artists in the process of creation. On the contrary, the artists' individual thoughts, feelings and styles as well as their observations of the features of real people are embodied in their works. Therefore, the supernatural Buddhas and deities appear somewhat human. The statues of historical figures especially resemble their respective features and distinct character. They look so lifelike that each has its own charm and people can easily distinguish one from another. Some statues are made of clay, some of bronze, and others are made of gold and silver. Certain commanding images are several metres high while some figurines are as delicate as pellets, which fully reveal the creative talent of the folk artists.

59. Buddha Phagpa Logeshari
This Buddhist image is enshrined in the Saint's Chapel (Phagpa Lhakhang), an early building in the Potala Palace. It was said to be the statue of the patron saint of Songtsan Gambo who asked the Nepalese for this statue to be worshipped. It is the dominant Buddhist image enshrined in the Palace. (1.18 metres high, sandalwood carving, c. 7th century)

60. King Songtsan Gambo

King Songtsan Gambo was an outstanding national hero in Tibetan history. As stated in historical records, 'Succeeding to the throne in his youth, he was a brave, wise, and resourceful king.' During his reign, he unified Tibet, which used to be a loosely knit and backward region, and established the powerful Tubo Dynasty. These accomplishments promoted socio-political, economic and cultural progress, and strengthened the unity between the Tibetan people and various nationalities of China. The Buddhists regard Songtsan Gambo as the incarnation of Boddhisattva Avalokitesvara. There is a small image of the Buddha of Infinite Light on his head, showing his worship of the Buddha. (1.55 metres high, clay figure, c. 7th century)

61. Princess Wen Cheng

The virtuous, beautiful, and versatile Princess Wen Cheng left an indelible impression on the minds of the Tibetan people. She lived in Tibet for 40 years. Many anecdotes about her life in Tibet are connected with the daily life and productive activities of the local people. Princess Wen Cheng died in 680 A.D. and a most grand funeral was held which was unprecedentedly recorded in the books of Tubo history. (1.11 metres high, clay figure, c. 7th century)

62. Gar Tongtsan

Gar Tongtsan was a Venerable minister assisting King Songtsan Gambo to found his dynasty. In 640 A.D. he was dispatched by Songtsan Gambo to Chang'an to escort Princess Wen Cheng to Tibet for the royal marriage. During the process, he manifested extraordinary wit and talent, which has become a sort of legend for posterity. (1.8 metres high, clay figure, c. 7th century)

64

63. Buddhist Images in the North Chapel in the West Hall

64. Tunmi Sangbuza

Tunmi Sangbuza was an illustrious writer who created the Tibetan language in the Tubo era. Having studied in India, he assimilated the characteristics of Sanskrit and the languages of various countries in Central Asia and formulated the Tibetan alphabet consisting of thirty simple letters. Later, he completed linguistic works such as *Thirty Rules of Grammar* and *Lexicological Structure*, thus making great contributions to the development of Tibetan culture. (1.75 metres high, clay figure, c. 7th century)

65. Statues of Sakyamuni (left) and the Fifth Dalai Lama

Sakyamuni, founder of Buddhism, was originally the son of King Gautama Suddhodana, ruler of Kapilavastu in ancient India (in present-day Nepal). According to legends, he gave up the comfortable life of a prince, left the palace for the wilderness to spiritually cultivate himself. Having lived as an ascetic for six years, he became the Buddha in the end. (2.28 metres high, pure gold, 17th century)

The 5th Dalai Lama, Ngawang Lobzang Gyatso (1617-1682), was a native of Qunjie County in Tibet. In 1652, he went to Beijing to pay respects to the Qing Emperor. In the following year, the Qing government conferred on him the official title Dalai Lama ('Dalai' means 'the sea' in Mongolian, 'Lama' means 'high priest' in Tibetan). Since then, all the succeeding Dalai Lamas were chosen, appointed and inaugurated by the central government. (2.55 metres, silver, 17th century)

66. Tsong Khapa

A native of Huangzhong County in Qinghai Province, Tsong Khapa was the founder of the Gelugpa Sect (Yellow Sect) of Lamaism. Like other Buddhist sects, this sect was patronized by the feudal central government in Beijing, and it gradually developed to be the dominant sect. (2.4 metres high, silver, 17th century)

67. Padma Sambhava

A Buddhist monk in ancient India. It was said that in the latter period of the 8th century, the Tubo king invited him to come to Tibet to exorcise demons. Later, he was venerated as the Founding Father of the Karmapa Sect (Red Sect) of Lamaism. (2.3 metres high, silver, 17th century)

68. White Goddess of Salvation

A seven-eyed goddess in mythology, she is one of the patron saints of longevity in the Tantric Sect of Buddhism. It is believed that she is able to read people's minds so that nothing escapes her. (1.4 metres high, gilt silver, 18th century)

69-70. Images of the Incarnations of Tsong Khapa
According to Buddhist doctrines, the Buddha is able to transfigure into all kinds of images called 'incarnations.' There are five graphic images of Tsong Khapa's incarnations exquisitely wrought. Here are two of them. (left: 0.47 metre high, right: 0.43 metre high, gilt bronze, 17th century)

69

70

**71. Bird Deity Garuda flanked by Serpent Goddesses
on the Apex of a Mandorla**
(Roc: 1.1 metre high, gilt bronze, 17th century)

72. Maitreya Buddha
The Maitreya Buddha is the Buddha of Future. This statue not only
displays the superb technique of metal smelting and artistic
moulding on the part of the Tibetan people, but also reveals the
characteristic of Tibetan handicrafts. (0.45 metre high, gilt bronze,
17th century)

Buddhist Scriptures

The Potala Palace boasts an ample collection of books kept in more than 20,000 cases. They cover a wide range of subjects such as religion, grammar, history, geography, biography, annals of temples, medicine, architecture, poetry, drama, etc. Of all the different kinds of books the Buddhist scriptures are the most voluminous.

It was believed that certain sutras had been translated during the reign of Songtsan Gambo. A good many sutras were further rendered into Tibetan from Chinese Buddhist scriptures with the approval of Khride Tsutsan. In the middle of the 8th century, as the dominant native religion (Bon) grew more and more influential and posed a greater threat to the Tobu court, King Khrisong Detsan strongly advocated Buddhism to counteract the native religion, thereby enhancing the translation of Buddhist scriptures on a larger scale. As listed in the Tangeh catalogue which is the only one extant, translated sutras in that period amount to 700 items or so. After prolonged and repeated struggles with the indigenous religion, Buddhism was deeply rooted in Tibet and developed into a kind of Tibetan Buddhism. Over a thousand years, it has infiltrated into the ideological and cultural spheres in the region with a far-reaching impact.

73. Part of the Sutra Collection

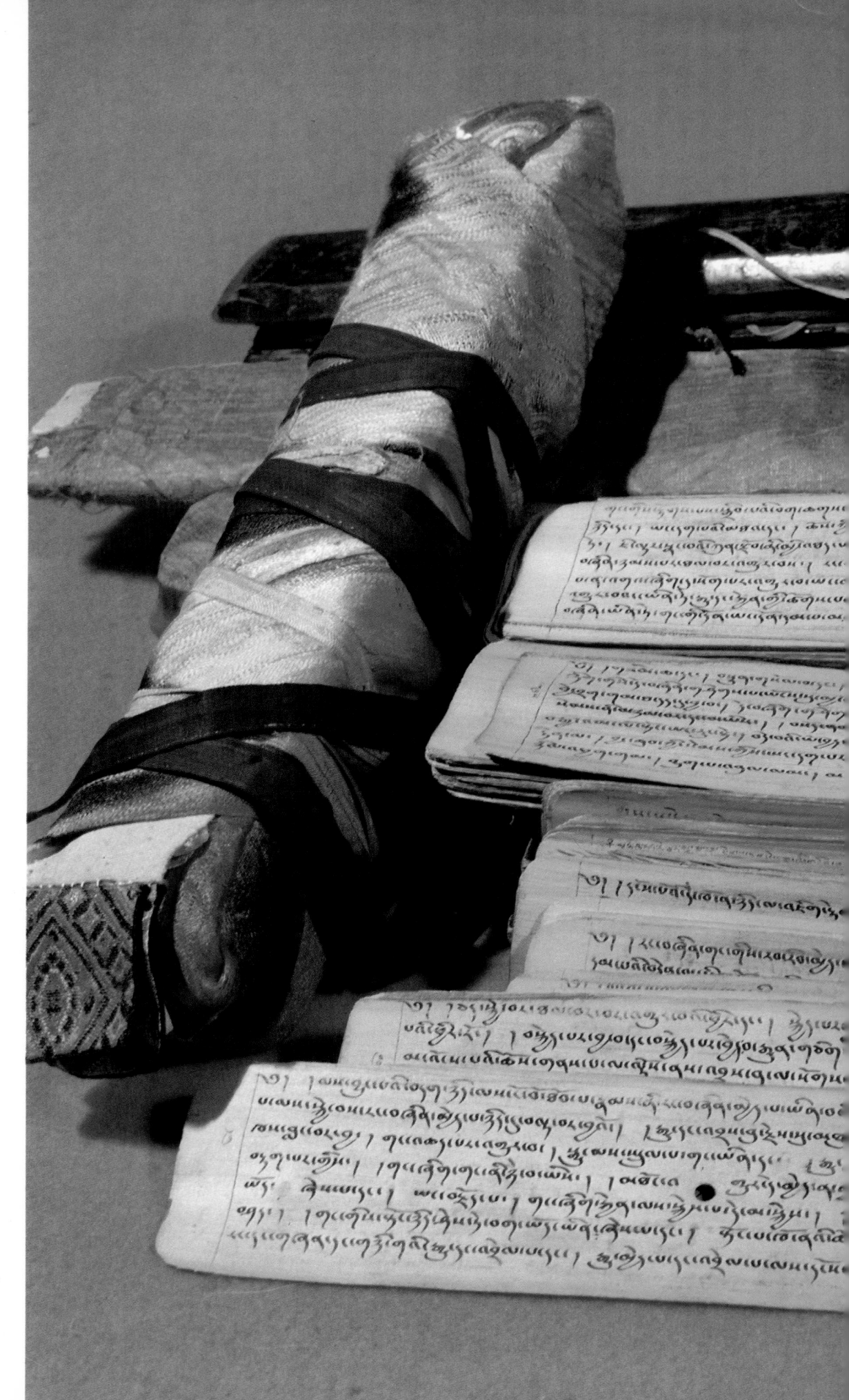

74. Pattra Scriptures

Buddhist scriptures written on palm leaves are very rare, so they are invaluable cultural relics as well as important historical data for studying the religion, culture and social system of antiquity.

75. The *Tripitaka*

The *Tripitaka* is an august collection of Buddhist canons. It is the
encyclopaedia of Buddhism. This picture shows the edition of
Kangyur granted by the Qing Emperor Yong Zheng. It is written
in golden letters, and, together with another part, *Tangyur*,
comprises the *Tripitaka* in the Tibetan language. The *Kangyur* is a
compilation of Sakyamuni's teachings expounded by the Buddha
himself. It chiefly elucidates Buddhist doctrines and disciplines. The
other part, *Tangyur*, consists of annotations and explanations with
miscellaneous information about medicine, astrology, history,
literature, language, arts and crafts, etc. It is, therefore, like an
encyclopaedia.

76. Researchers Sorting Out and Investigating the Sutra Collection

Chortens

Chorten Halls are the principal structure in the Red Palace where the remains of successive generations of Dalai Lamas are preserved. In the Palace there are altogether eight chortens, each for the remains of one of the following Dalai Lamas: the 5th Dalai Lama, Ngawang Lobzang Gyatso; the 7th Dalai Lama, Keizang Gyatso; the 8th Dalai Lama, Jampei Gyatso; the 9th Dalai Lama, Longto Gyatso; the 10th Dalai Lama, Tshutrim Gyatso; the 11th Dalai Lama, Khedru Gyatso; the 12th Dalai Lama, Chinlei Gyatso; and the 13th Dalai Lama, Thutan Gyatso.

Chortens of various Dalai Lamas are of the same form but in different sizes. They had been built with a lavish expenditure of money and man power. The chortens are coated with gold coverings, hence they are also called gold chortens in the annals. Studded all over with pearls, jewels and precious stones, they look exceedingly magnificent.

It was recorded that over 18,000 taels of gold were spent to coat the chorten of the 13th Dalai Lama, and that of the 5th Dalai Lama cost more than 110,000 taels of gold. The jewels and precious stones used for the same purpose cost even 10 times as much as the gold spent.

78. Chorten
Coated with gold and inlaid with pearls and jewels, the chortens are fabulously luxurious. Each chorten is divided into three parts: the top, the main structure and the base. This photo shows the chorten of the 11th Dalai Lama.

79. The 'Window'
This is the 'window' of the chorten containing the remains of the 13th Dalai Lama, behind which is the main structure preserving the body.

80. The Base of a Chorten with Sacrifices
Built in 1930, the chorten containing the remains of the 13th Dalai Lama is 14 metres high, studded all over with pearls, jade and jewellery.

79

80

81

81. Gawu (Amulet Box)
Set in the chorten as a decoration, this kind of Gawu is a precious
ornament worn by Tibetan women.

82. Dragon Decorating the Base of a Chorten

83-84. Dragons and
Phoenixes in Bas-relief
on a Chorten

84

85. A Three-dimensional Pearl and Coral Mandala Offering
Placed in the chorten hall of the 13th Dalai Lama, the pearl mandra
is strung with more than 200,000 pieces of pearl and coral.

86. A Three-dimensional Pearl and Coral Mandala Offering

Golden
Roofs

87. One of the Golden Roofs
Every chorten hall of a renowned Dalai Lama is topped with a
golden roof. This photo shows such a roof on the chorten hall of
the 13th Dalai Lama.

88. Groups of Golden Roofs

89

89-95. Different
Views of the
Golden Roofs

90

92

110

95

96

96. At the Top
97. A Panoramic View of Lhasa

Appendices

Plan of the Potala Palace

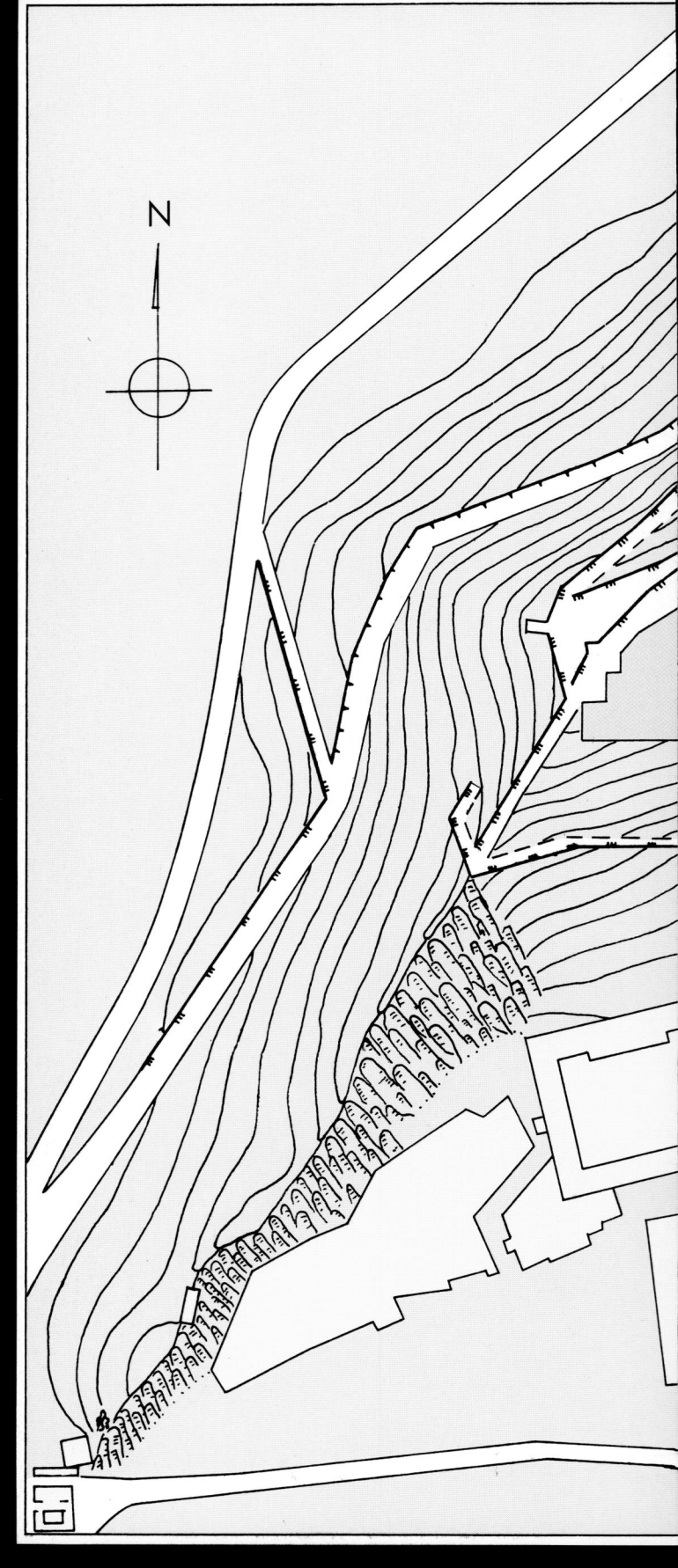

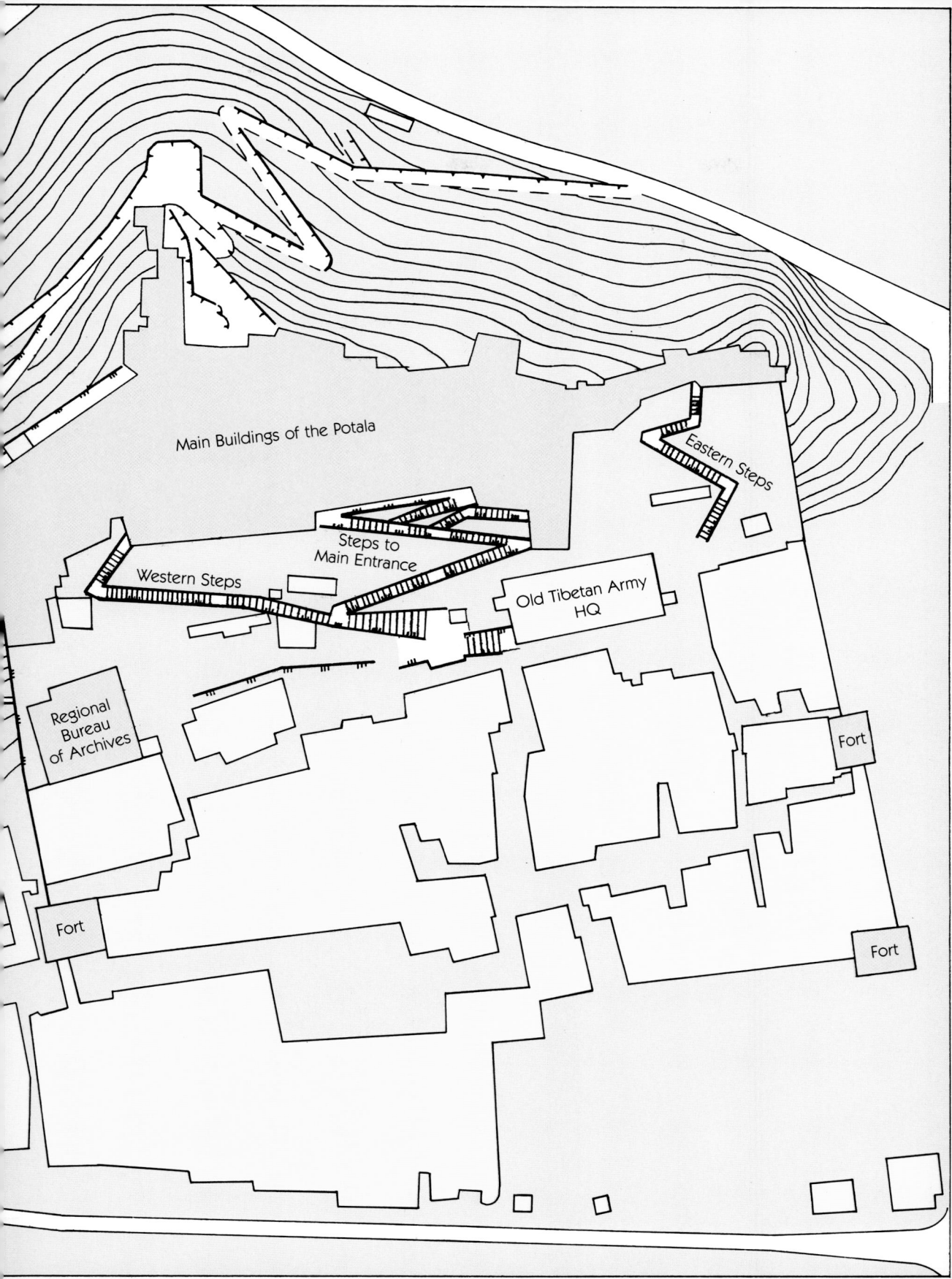

Main Buildings of the Potala

Eastern Steps

Steps to
Main Entrance

Western Steps

Old Tibetan Army
HQ

Regional
Bureau
of Archives

Fort

Fort

Fort

Chronology

634 A.D. Horse year, 8th year of Zhen Guan, Tang dynasty

Mission sent by Songtsan Gambo, Tsanpo (king) of Tibet, arrived at Chang'an and requested for a marriage between the Tibetan king and a princess of Tang. Emperor of Tang sent in return a mission to Lhasa.

At the beginning of the 7th century, Songtsan Gambo removed his seat of government to Lhasa as the ruler of Tibet.

641 Ox year, 15th year of Zhen Guan, Tang dynasty

Arrival of Princess Wen Cheng from Tang. Songtsan Gambo built for her the first palace on Marpo Ri, the Red Hill, at Lhasa.

710 Dog year, 1st year of Jing Yun, Tang dynasty

Arrival of Princess Jin Cheng from Tang to be wedded to Tsanpo Khride Tsutsan.

755 Sheep year, 14th year of Tian Bao, Tang dynasty

Accession of Tsanpo Khrisong Detsan. During his reign, the palace on Marpo Ri was once damaged by lightning.

842 Year of Male Water Dog, 2nd year of Hui Chang, Tang dynasty

Assassination of Darma, the last Tsanpo, and the end of the Tubo dynasty. Palace on Marpo Ri completely destroyed during a general uprising.

1645 Year of Female Wood Cock, 2nd year of Shun Zhi, Qing dynasty

Building of the White Palace of Potala on Marpo Ri begun by the 5th Dalai Lama, Lobzang Gyatso (1617-1682). It was completed in 1648.

1653 Year of Female Water Snake, 10th year of Shun Zhi, Qing dynasty

Emperor Shun Zhi of Qing conferred by royal rescript the title of 'The Great Benevolent Self-Existent Buddha of Western Paradise, Overseer of the Buddhist Faith under the Heaven, the All-knowing Vadjradhara Dalai Lama' on Lobzang Gyatso. The 5th Dalai Lama moved from Gandan Phodrang in Drepung monastery to the palace of Potala.

1690 Year of Male Iron Horse, 29th year of Kang Xi, Qing dynasty

Building of the Red Palace of Potala and the 5th Dalai Lama's chorten begun by Depa (Chief Administrator) Sanggye Gyatso. Building completed in 1693.

1697 Year of Female Fire Ox, 36th year of Kang Xi, Qing dynasty
Installation of the 6th Dalai Lama, Tshangyang Gyatso (1683-1706)

1706 Year of Male Fire Dog, 45th year of Kang Xi, Qing dynasty
Lhazang Khan of the Qosot Mongols killed Sanggye Gyatso and deposed the 6th Dalai Lama. Rival candidate Yeshi Gyatso installed at Potala as Dalai Lama.
1709 Emperor Kang Xi sent a minister for peaceful settlement.

1717 The Jungar Mongols raided Lhasa and killed Lhazang Khan.

1718-1719 Emperor Kang Xi sent armies to repel the Jungars and restored peace and order in Tibet.

1720 Year of Male Iron Mouse, 59th year of Kang Xi, Qing dynasty
Installation of the 7th Dalai Lama, Keizang Gyatso (1708-1757) at Potala.

1762 Year of Male Water Horse, 27th year of Qian Long, Qing dynasty
Installation of the 8th Dalai Lama, Jampei Gyatso (1758-1804) at Potala.

1808 Year of Male Earth Dragon, 13th year of Jia Qing, Qing dynasty
Installation of the 9th Dalai Lama, Longto Gyatso (1805-1815) at Potala.

1822 Year of Male Earth Horse, 2nd year of Dao Guang, Qing dynasty
Installation of Tshutrim Gyatso (1816-1837) at Potala as the 10th Dalai Lama after drawing of lots from the Gold Urn in Lhasa.

1842 Year of Male Earth Tiger, 22nd year of Dao Guang, Qing dynasty
Installation of Khedru Gyatso (1838-1855) as the 11th Dalai Lama after drawing of lots from the Gold Urn in Lhasa.

1858 Year of Male Earth Horse, 8th year of Xian Feng, Qing dynasty
Installation of Chinlei Gyatso (1856-1875) as the 12th Dalai Lama after drawing of lots from the Gold Urn in Lhasa.

1878 Year of Male Earth Tiger, 4th year of Guang Xu, Qing dynasty
Installation of the 13th Dalai Lama, Thutan Gyatso (1876-1933) at Potala.

1904 Year of Male Wood Dragon, 30th year of Guang Xu, Qing dynasty
Signing of the 'Lhasa Convention' at Potala after British invasion to Lhasa.

1934 Year of Male Wood Dog, 23rd year of Republic of China
Condolence and posthumous honours to the late 13th Dalai Lama conveyed by Chief Commissioner of the Commission on Mongolian and Tibetan Affairs. Building of the 13th Dalai Lama's chorten begun at Potala. It was completed in 1936.

1940 Year of Male Iron Dragon, 29th year of Republic of China
Installation of the 14th Dalai Lama, Tandzin Gyatso (1935-) under supervision of Chief Commissioner of the Commission on Mongolian and Tibetan Affairs.

1951 Year of Female Iron Hare
Signing of agreement on measures for the peaceful liberation of Tibet on May 23, 1951 by representatives of the Central People's Government and delegates of the local government of Tibet. Liberation of Tibet.

Compiled by Chang Fengxuan

Born in Yuci, Shanxi in 1927, Chang Fengxuan is of the Han nationality.

He once studied in China University and in Peking University and graduated from the National Minority Languages Department of the Central Nationalities College.

He is now an assistant research fellow of the Nationality Research Institute of the Chinese Academy of Social Science.